D0313800

ERLEIT N 1 4 OCT 2008

WAVERLEY

PORTRAIT OF A FAMOUS ROUTE

ROGER SIVITER

Published by
Runpast Publishing
10 Kingscote Grove, Cheltenham, Glos GL51 6JX

1. *Above:* A true winter's day on the Waverley route as Class 'V2' 2-6-2 No. 60824 slogs up the 1 in 75 gradient between Steele Road and Riccarton Junction in a snow-storm.
  The date is 4 December 1965 and the train is the 2.12 pm Carlisle Kingmoor-Edinburgh Millerhill goods. *Mick York*

© Roger Siviter &
Runpast Publishing
ISBN 1 870754 38 7
October 1996

Printed by:
The Amadeus Press Ltd.,
Leeds Road,
Huddersfield,
West Yorkshire

SCOTTISH BORDERS LIBRARY SERVICE

ACCESSION No.	CLASS No.
253346	335.09413

SCOTTISH
BORDERS
LIBRARY
SERVICE

INTRODUCTION

The Waverley route, together with the Somerset & Dorset Railway, is perhaps the most sadly missed of all the lines that were closed in the 'Beeching Era' of the 1960s.

Running through some of the most beautiful scenery in the British Isles, the Waverley served the people of the border counties for more than a hundred years until its closure in 1969.

Travelling on the line in the 1960s I for one have never failed to be thrilled by the climb up to Whitrope, the charm of the stations, the beauty of Gala Water and the many other aspects of this beautiful line all of which combined to give the feeling that you were travelling on one of the great railway routes of the British Isles.

Our journey begins in Carlisle and the period is from the late 1940s until the closure of the line.

Many North British Locomotives are featured as well as the fine LNER locomotives designed by Sir Nigel Gresley. In the latter years a few LMS classes were to be seen on the line and these are also shown together with some of the BR standard steam and diesel classes which appeared in the closing years of the line.

In compiling this book I have been very fortunate in having so many people who have been willing and able to help me and I should like to take this opportunity to thank them all.

To the photographers who have let me choose from their picture collections and when necessary let me make prints from their precious negatives.

To Neil Caplan for the splendid historical notes.

To Ken Hale, Dave Lacey, Stuart Sellar, Mick York, Chris Weston and Patrick Whitehouse for much help and advice.

To Joan Wappett for the typing and my wife Christina for the maps and help with the layout.

To Rae Montgomery for suggesting amendments and Bob Lynn for providing new photographs for this edition.

Lastly but most of all to the professional railwaymen who ran the Waverley I say thank you for making it a truly great and memorable route.

Roger Siviter

2. *Right:* Gone but not forgotten.
David E. Gouldthorp

HISTORICAL BACKGROUND

In Britain we have been fortunate in our railways — and this not only in the economic context. This statement may seem provocative to people who think of railways as among the 'predators' of the landscape, the forerunners of pylons and motorways. In fact, however, many of the nineteenth century lines did not scar permanently the natural setting and their major structures have merged in so well down the years.

The Waverley route was just such a railway and its natural setting was glorious indeed. Much as I came under the spell of the Waverley route, I must not claim for it quite the same grandeur as that of the Highland Railway's mainline from Perth to Inverness, or that of so much of the West Highland line and the Kyle line. Where the Waverley route can fairly be said to have scored was in that rich variety of landscapes over the 98¼ miles from the Firth of Forth through the Southern Uplands to Solway Firth. The Waverley route could also more than hold its own when it came to historical and romantic associations even though there was no single episode which matched altogether the drama and tragedy of the 'Forty-Five' for the West Highlands and the Stuarts in the 'territory' of the West Highland line. The Border country had witnessed many centuries of bitter conflict between the two Kingdoms, as well as of scarcely less bitter local conflicts. These left indelible marks in the stories, legends and poetry of the Borders long before Sir Walter Scott brought his genius to bear upon this heritage.

The beginnings of the Waverley route were not spectacular and it took virtually a generation before it came fully into operation as part of an Anglo-Scottish trunk route. Its history is essentially that of the North British Railway — a very great British Railway.

Although the completion in 1846 of the Edinburgh & Berwick line had seemed to point the North British to the East Coast for a share in Anglo-Scottish traffics, in the event its major interest developed south-westwards to Carlisle. The vital first step in this direction came in 1849 with the opening of the Edinburgh & Hawick Railway but it took a further 13 years to reach Carlisle. The East Coast through route was completed in 1850 with the opening of the two great bridges, The Royal Border Bridge at Berwick-upon-Tweed and the High Level Bridge at Newcastle-upon-Tyne. The North British and the North Eastern Railways were partners of course in the East Coast route but for long they were distinctly uneasy bedfellows. The North British had its fears of being forced into amalgamation with the North Eastern and the latter company strongly resented what it saw as the North British 'intrusion' into Northumberland.

The situation south of Hawick changed greatly towards the end of the 1850s. The Border Union Railway from Hawick to Carlisle was under construction and the Border Counties Railway was completed from Hexham to Riccarton to join the Border Union line. By 1860 the North British Railway had effective control of the Border counties and was eager to move closer to the Tyne. The Border Union line reached Carlisle in 1862 but the same year saw another highly important development: the key Newcastle & Carlisle Railway was absorbed by the North Eastern Railway. This checked the North British at Hexham and left it facing there the very company with which it was so often at odds. The North British and the North Eastern did reach an agreement which gave the former running rights between Hexham and Newcastle but in return the North Eastern obtained the much larger benefit of running rights from

Berwick to Edinburgh. As the North Eastern insisted on the full use of these powers the role of the North British in the operation of the East Coast route was greatly diminished over the next 30 years.

It became a matter of the utmost importance for the future of the North British Railway to try to develop the Waverley route in full partnership with an English company as part of an alternative Anglo-Scottish trunk route. The Midland Railway was the only possible partner in this because the London & North Western and the Caledonian Railways were so firmly allied in the operation of the West Coast route. The problem was that the Midland Railway had access to Carlisle — and thus to the Waverley route — only by grace of the London & North Western Railway. The Midland's own 'railhead' was still at Ingleton and the LNWR owned the line running north to join the West Coast route at Low Gill.

Everything depended therefore on the Midland Railway building a line of its own to Carlisle. After some hesitation the Midland went ahead with the tremendous and so-costly task of building the Settle & Carlisle line. This was opened for passenger traffic in 1876 — fourteen years after the North British Railway had reached Carlisle. At last, the Waverley route could come into its own. From 1876 to 1914 the North British and the Midland competed seriously with the East and West Coast routes for a good share of Anglo-Scottish traffics. It is true that their route had the drawback of being longer — 23 miles more to Edinburgh than over the East Coast route (when trains called at Nottingham and Sheffield en route). This made it impracticable for the allies to offer the faster journey but they provided an excellent service of 'Corridor Express' trains. The Midland and the North British set and maintained the highest standards of passenger comfort and catering in the Anglo-Scottish travel. The superior scenic and historical interest of the Waverley route proved to be a decided attraction for those travellers who were not seeking simply the quickest journey to and from Scotland.

The Waverley route was always a tough and challenging line for the steam locomotives and crews, particularly during the many severe winters. The northern summit at Falahill (880 ft) was stiff enough to surmount but the southern summit at Whitrope (1006 ft) involved ten miles of 1:70 and Whitrope had an epic quality. The 'Corridor Express' continued to increase in weight and demanded periodically the building of more powerful locomotives. The North British Railway provided a succession of admirable engines, beginning with the '420' class 4-4-0 by Wheatley in 1873 and Dugald Drummond's '476' class 4-4-0 of 1876-78. The culminating point in locomotive design and performance came in 1906-11 with Reid's superb 'Atlantic' class — these engines put up so many magnificent runs over the Waverley route with heavy trains worked at high speed, taking into account the severe gradients and the extreme curvature of the route. Though Reid did not design his famous 'Scott' class 4-4-0 of 1909 for working the Waverley route, and these engines did not come to it in numbers until the 1920s, it would be unfair not to give them mention here. The 'Scotts' gave some 30 years of excellent service to the route and they became so closely identified with it that it seemed almost as if they had been there always!

Understandably, railway enthusiasts drawn to the express passenger service over the Waverley route but the *Waverley* was part of the daily life of the Border country and for most of its existence was vital for the wellbeing of the population. The passenger service was designed to give an excellent service to the towns along the Route: Galashiels, Melrose, Hawick together with St. Boswells as the important junction station for several branch lines. In 1914 the smallest stations were served by stopping trains between Edinburgh and Hawick and between Hawick and Carlisle. There was even a Sunday service between Edinburgh and Hawick.

For its length, the Waverley route had a good many branch lines. Modest as most of these were, all gave valuable service for passengers and freight before road transport eventually came to offer an alternative. Space makes it impossible for me to do more than list these branches — as they were in 1914 and taking them from the north. Fountainhall-Lauder (10½ miles), Galashiels-Selkirk (6¼ miles), Galashiels-Peebles (this was really a 'round' with the northern arm between Hardengreen junction, Leadburn and Peebles), St. Boswells-Reston (30¾ — the former 'Berwickshire Railway'), St. Boswells-Kelso and Berwick (35 to Berwick), St. Boswells-Jedburgh, via Roxburgh (15½ in all), Riccarton Junction-Hexham (42), Riddings-Langholm (7), and finally, the almost totally-forgotten Longtown-Gretna (3¼) which lost its passenger service in 1915!

Soon after the 1914-18 war, the Grouping took place and unhappily the Waverley route began to lose out to the East and West Coast routes. Initially, the Waverley gained a 'titled train' in 1927 with the *Thames-Forth Express*. At that time the rival routes had not begun their fierce competition over journey times and the schedule of the *Thames-Forth Express* compared well with that of the *Flying Scotsman*. The latter had 8 hr 15 min against the 8 hr 40 min of the *Thames-Forth* but its journey was only 392.9 miles whereas the *Thames-Forth* had to cover 416 miles. But the position changed materially after 1932 with the big reductions in journey times over the East and West Coast routes. By 1937, the *Flying Scotsman* was reaching Edinburgh in 7 hr only — with its world-famous nonstop run. This opened up an impossible gap for the Waverley route and it was inevitable that the status of the Waverley would be further diminished. The outbreak of war in 1939 disguised this for many years however.

Nationalisation came in 1947 and brought with it 'rationalisation' in so many spheres. Resources were limited and these were concentrated on the East and West Coast routes. The Waverley route suffered from these changes but so much remained in the 1960s to remind one of former glories — and of the North British itself even though formally it had departed in 1923. There was also the added interest of far more freight traffic being moved over the route with the linking of those great new marshalling yards at Edinburgh Millerhill and Carlisle Kingmoor.

The battle to save the Waverley route was hard-fought and gallant. It was lost eventually and a Great British railway route died in January 1969. Yes, the Waverley route has passed into history but it is a wonderful tribute to its very special character, and its fine achievements that so many people still recall it with warm interest and affection.

Neil Caplan

3. Class 'B1' 4-6-0 No. 61221 *Sir Alexander Erskine-Hill* pulls out of Carlisle Citadel station with an afternoon Waverley route local train. Although the locomotive has a BR number, it is still in LNER green with LNER lettering on the tender which would date this picture around 1949/50. Note the gallows type signal (partly obscured by smoke) to the right of the train. *Eric Treacy/Millbrook House*

CONTENTS

CARLISLE — RICCARTON JUNCTION

The southern half of the Waverley route, Carlisle to Hawick, began as the Border Union Railway. It opened for goods on 23 June 1862 and passengers on 1 July, and gave the North British Railway Company a foothold in the Caledonian's Carlisle Citadel station. This was achieved by circuitous means, which explains the Waverley's strange changes of direction. The NB leased the thirteen mile long Silloth Bay & Docks Company line, and bought it in 1880, which looped round the west side of Citadel station. It generated lucrative freight traffic from Dundee and Leith to Silloth for shipment to Liverpool, Dublin, etc. The NB also leased the Port Carlisle Railway, a two and a half mile spur from Drumburgh junction on the Silloth line, with its running rights over the short length of Caledonian metals into the north end of Citadel. This railway was famous for its horse-drawn 'dandy' carriages. It closed in 1932.

The Silloth line continued its avoiding loop south and east, through Denton Holme (former goods) and to Petteril junction, there meeting the line from Newcastle (NER) and the Midland line from Settle, which opened in 1876 and ran into Citadel from the south east. By its alliance with the Midland Railway, the NB enjoyed direct passenger traffic through the Caledonian station, besides the goods traffic via the loop through Denton Holme. The station was rebuilt in its Gothic form in 1876 to accommodate the increase in traffic, and modernised in the 1950s.

The Waverley route started under the golden sandstone of Citadel Tower, then ran under a decorative street bridge and past Carlisle No 4 box on the left. After the A595 crossed the line by the Castle, the line hugged the River Caldew; its junction of that name gave onto a line running south to Denton Holme. Once over the river, the line passed through Port Carlisle Branch junction by Carlisle No 3 box. Here the ex-Caledonian line continued to Glasgow via Beattock, while the ex-NB line swung sharply southwest on the original Port Carlisle track, crossing the canal which cut off a great loop of the River Eden. At Canal junction it met the Silloth line under the imposing four-storied box: the Waverley swung north enclosing a marshalling yard on the right, while the Silloth line branched off west. Although the seaward end was dismantled in the 1960s, the first few hundred yards remained leading to Canal shed. After this closed in 1963 its motive power transferred to the ex-Caledonian Kingmoor shed. From Canal junction the Silloth line also branched south to Carlisle No 1 box at Willow Holme junction, and thence to Denton Holme.

The line crossed the River Eden on a red sandstone viaduct under the power pylons, ran through Stainton level crossing, and rose to cross the Glasgow line with Kingmoor sheds down on the right and the marshalling yards on the left. Spurs dropped down to these yards before the bridge. After Brunthill box on the left, it ran through Parkhouse Halt for the RAF depot with its box and spur on the left, and through Harker station, which was closed to passengers in 1929, but enjoyed a wartime revival. The next level crossing with its box on the left served Lyneside station, which was closed in 1929. The route crossed the River Lyne, with a view over the Solway Flats: the River Esk to the west is constrained from flooding by embankments. After Fauldmoor level crossing at Hopesike Woods, on what had been an island in the marshes, stands a church with a long nave and a short stump of a tower. Trains used to reach 70 mph on this flat straight stretch.

The line crossed the Esk on Longtown viaduct by a gravel pit and the A7 bridge; since Roman times this was a strategic point on the Border. The battle of Solway Moss was fought nearby in 1542. On the north bank a single track ran three and a quarter miles west to link with the Glasgow line, joining it at Gretna South junction (formerly Border Union junction). This line was opened in 1862 and ran to the NB station at Gretna. The NB and the Glasgow & South Western were granted running rights on the twenty-four chains of Caledonian track between Gretna South and Gretna junctions. There was a yard at Gretna Green for the NB and the G & SW to exchange goods, there being no facility at Carlisle.

Immediately after this junction and signalbox on the left was the level crossing at Longtown station, and beyond it near Oakbank, some sheds and sidings. The line squeezed between the Esk and the A7 for a mile to Scotch Dyke station, spelt the English way, with its box on the right, close to Scots Dyke which was thrown up after the Border Settlement. The edge of its canopy bore the motto 'Speed and Comfort by Rail'. This station was closed in 1949. The level crossing beyond led to Kirkandrews-on-Esk, a church built in Renaissance style, whose tower is topped by a dome supported by columns.

The route re-crossed the Esk on the Thistle viaduct, a plate girder bridge on stone columns, then, under the tower of Liddel Strength, it followed the tributary Liddel Water which marked the Scottish Border. At Riddings station, with its box on the right, a junction served a seven mile track to Langholm to the north. Before the Waverley route was built, the Caledonian proposed a rival single track route passing through Langholm; naturally the NB had to offer a rail link to this busy little town. It crossed the Esk on a splendid viaduct of golden stone arches, and was opened on 18 April 1864. The branch and Riddings station were closed on 18 September 1967. It was here, too, that a symbolic length of Waverley track was lifted on Monday 6 January 1969.

Penton bank rose four miles at 1 in 100 up Liddesdale to the substantial station house at Penton, with the box just beyond on the right. On Chamot Hill to the east, a fire-watch tower guarded Kershope Forest, and Tinnisburn Forest to the north. The line continued past a neat little suspension footbridge and Stonehouse Tower in one of the many loops in the river, and crossed the Scottish Border at Kershopefoot station, with the box on the left controlling the level crossing. The Border follows Kershope Burn northeast to Caplestone Fell, while the Waverley route swung northward. On this easier stretch, trains often managed 60 mph.

The line crossed Liddel Water by the weir at Milnholm Cross, passed under the B6357 and came onto the flat area of Newcastleton. This was founded in the late 17th Century when the then Duke of Buccleuch resettled the inhabitants of Castleton, a village near Liddel Castle. This important new town served a large area, for schooling, worship and revelry. The level crossing by the station was the setting for the drama when the very last train ran, the 9.55 pm Waverley—St. Pancras Night Midland sleeper of Sunday 5 January 1969, when the minister with his parishioners padlocked the crossing gates and blocked the line for an hour.

Through trains often achieved 55 mph, but in a mile the gradient steepened from 1 in 200 to 1 in 125, and the next eight miles to Whitrope summit were mostly 1 in 75, where trains were lucky to maintain 30 mph. The line crossed the confluence of Hermitage Water on Sandholm viaduct, built of grey whinstone arches which had no parapet, only a handrail. It turned northeast and passed Liddel Castle. The original Castleton cemetery could be seen on top of the east bank by the road, under the wooded slopes of Newcastleton Forest. The line climbed out onto open moorlands, and a couple of miles brought it to the windswept single storey station at Steele Road set in a cluster of pine trees with its box by the 'down' line. The line crossed the lane for Hermitage, and finally left Liddel Water near the 67 mile post, swinging northwest up to the watershed between the rivers of the Solway and those of the Teviot and Tweed. As it rounded Arnton Fell, 1464ft high, passing under the two much-photographed occupation bridges, it came in sight of Riccarton Junction.

From the east around Shiel Knowe on the 1425 ft high Saughtree Fell ran the single track line from Hexham via Reedsmouth junction. This was the NB Border Counties Railway which opened at the same time as the Waverley, linking with the Newcastle & Carlisle Railway at Hexham. it was first promoted by W H Charlton of Hesleyside to carry coal from the Plashetts mines in Northumberland to the woollen mills of the Tweed valley, and was originally planned to run to Hawick. When the NER bought up the N & CR, the then chairman of NB, Richard Hodgson, had to bargain for running rights, conceding reciprocal rights to the NER on the NB's East Coast route from Edinburgh to Berwick on Tweed. Although the passenger service finished on 15 October 1956 and the last freight trains ran to Reedsmouth, from Morpeth, in 1963, a few hundred yards near the junction were retained for storing stock.

Riccarton Junction was a railway community of some hundred and twenty people in thirty cottages. They were served by daily deliveries by rail to the 'Riccarton Grocery Branch Hawick Co-op Society' shop on the platform. Next to it was the sub-post office and telephone kiosk, while the refreshment room doubled as a pub. Three times a week there was a late stopper from Hawick for those returning from the cinema. It had a single schoolroom and teacher for juniors, while older children went to Newcastleton or Hawick in a single carriage often coupled to a regular freight. There was no doctor or minister, a light engine bringing one in emergency; coffins were carried free to Newcastleton or Hawick. Riccarton Junction was infamous in its early years because of a gang of four wives who terrorised the settlement. This problem was finally solved by transferring the employees, and their wives, to other areas of the country.

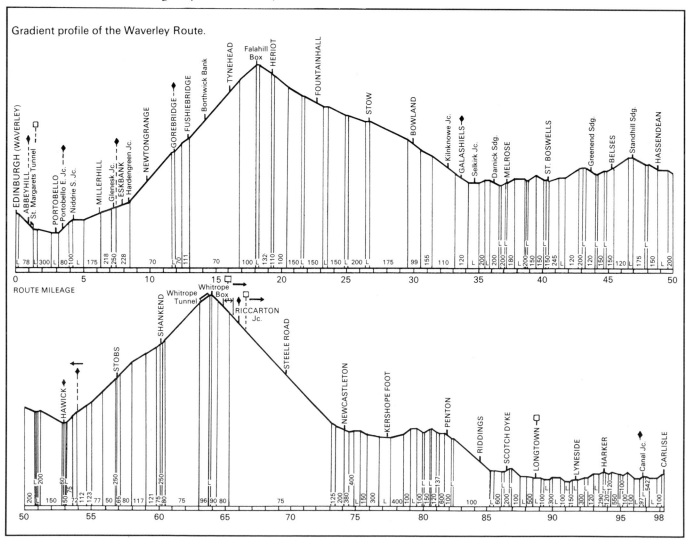

Gradient profile of the Waverley Route.

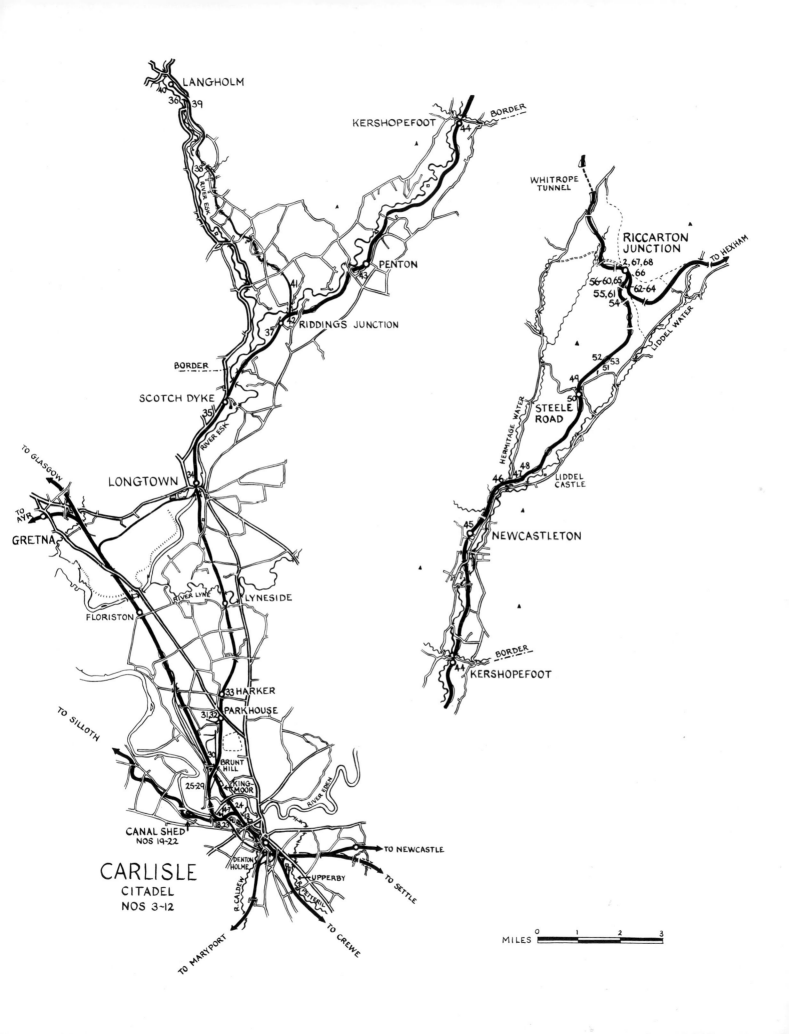

6. *Above:* On the early evening of 30 March 1966 Class '2MT' 2-6-2T No. 41217 is seen shunting a GPO van at the northern end of Citadel station. This class of tank locomotive was introduced in 1946 and designed by Ivatt. *Roger Siviter*

4. *Top left:* Our journey starts at the aptly named Carlisle Citadel station on a fine spring evening — 24 April 1961. Class 'D49' 4-4-0 No. 62711 *Dumbartonshire* waits to depart with the 6.13 pm local to Hawick. Alongside is the 6.20 pm DMU to Silloth. *Robert Leslie*

5. *Bottom left:* Class 'A2' Pacific No. 60519 *Honeyway* waits to depart from Carlisle with an Edinburgh train in the mid 1950s. This was the most powerful of all the LNER Pacifics having a tractive effort of 40,430 lb. In the background a BR standard Class 5MT No. 73056 is busy shunting stock. *Eric Treacy/Millbrook House*

7. *Right:* On 30 June 1963 Class '6P5F' 4-6-2 No. 72006 *Clan Mackenzie* prepares to leave Carlisle with a northbound train on the WCML. 'Coronation' Class Pacific No. 46249 *City of Sheffield* waits in the centre road. Both these classes of locomotives were to be seen on occasions on the Waverley route, mainly on diversion traffic. *Hugh Ballantyne*

8. *Top left:* A vintage LNER scene at Carlisle as Class 'A3' Pacific No. 99 *Call Boy* poses for the camera. The date is probably around 1946/47. Note the splendid 'Victorian Gothic' style of architecture which was sadly later replaced. *Eric Treacy/Millbrook House*

9. *Bottom left:* Class 'A3' Pacific No. 60096 *Papyrus* arrives at Carlisle with the 'up' *Waverley* on 27 February 1960. *Robert Leslie*

10. *Above:* A 1952 picture of 4-6-2 No. 60093 *Coronach* making a splendid exit from Carlisle with a Waverley route train. It looks like a case of smoke by arrangement! *Eric Treacy/Millbrook House*

11. Haymarket (64B) 'A2' Pacific No. 60519 *Honeyway* prepares to leave Citadel station with the 'down' *Waverley* in the late 1950s. On the left is 'Jinty' 0-6-0T No. 47354. These splendid little tank locomotives, of Midland Railway design, were a familiar sight in and around Carlisle station for many years. *Eric Treacy/Millbrook House*

12. The sleek lines of 'A4' Pacific No. 60009 *Union of South Africa* (happily now preserved in Scotland) glow in the winter sunshine as it pulls out of Carlisle with the 1.28 pm to Edinburgh, on 5 November 1960. 'A4s' were not regular performers on the Waverley, the bulk of the top link passenger work being handled by 'A3' Pacifics. *Robert Leslie*

13. Class 'D49' 4-4-0 No. 62712 *Morayshire* (also preserved in Scotland) seems in a hurry as it passes Carlisle No. 3 box with the 6.30 am local from Hawick in April 1961. At this location the Waverley route left the West Coast main line and headed westwards for about a mile before turning to the north and crossing over the WCML at Kingmoor. *S. C. Crook*

14. A splendid railway scene as Class '4MT' 2-6-4T No. 42440 leaves the LMS main line to Scotland at Port Carlisle junction in August 1961 with the 4.47 pm train to Silloth. No. 42440 was one of the ex LMS 2-6-4 tank locomotives transferred, around this time, to the former LNER shed at Carlisle Canal. The former North British Railway branch to Silloth (one of the Waverley route branches) was closed in the early 1960s. *S. C. Crook*

15 and 16. Two views of the 1.28 pm to Edinburgh as they pass Carlisle No. 1 box. In the top view 'A3' Pacific No. 60087 *Blenheim* (complete with double chimney and German type smoke deflectors) is seen in April 1961. In the bottom view, taken in February 1962, the train is hauled by 'Britannia' Pacific No. 70018 *Flying Dutchman*. This locomotive was built in 1951 and first shedded at Old Oak Common but finished its days at Carlisle Kingmoor shed. The reign of the Britannias was short lived on the Waverley route, the constant curvature of the route causing excessive tyre wear. *Two Pictures Peter J. Robinson*

17. The 6.13 pm stopping train to Hawick with 4-4-0 No. 62744 *The Holderness* in charge passes Carlisle No. 1 box on a beautiful August evening in 1960. *S. C. Crook*

18. Former NBR 0-6-0 Class 'J36' No. 65312, is caught by the camera on 16 July 1962 as it passes the splendid signal box at Canal junction. The entrance to Canal shed is to the left of the locomotive. The locomotive is on the Waverley route which swings away northwards at this junction. In the foreground are the tracks of the Silloth branch. *W. S. Sellar*

19. *Top left:* 'A3' Pacific No. 60068 *Sir Visto* poses in Canal shed on a Sunday in May 1963. This locomotive was fitted with a double chimney in 1959 but unlike many other members of this famous class was never fitted with smoke deflectors. *Peter J. Robinson*

20. *Bottom left:* A bird's eye view of Canal shed in June 1963 shortly before the shed closed on the 19th of that month. 'A4' No. 60012, 'A3' No. 60100, 'V2' No. 60816, 'B1' No. 61099 and 'Britannia' Pacific No. 70020 are amongst the locomotives that are visible. *Peter J. Robinson*

21. *Above:* Former LMS 2-6-4T No. 42210 complete with Canal shed code (12C) is seen on Canal shed in this view taken in 1961. Many former LMS 2-6-4 tanks were transferred to this shed around this period. *Peter J. Robinson*

22. *Below:* When the former LNER Canal shed was closed in 1963 many of the former LNER locomotives were serviced at Carlisle Kingmoor shed. In this picture we see 'A3' No. 60106 *Flying Fox* (by then withdrawn) coupled to the famous 'A4' Pacific No. 60007 *Sir Nigel Gresley,* which is still happily with us. The date is 1 January 1966. *Peter J. Robinson*

23. *Top left:* On 16 July 1962 'A2' Pacific No. 60534 *Irish Elegance* pulls out of Canal junction yard with a 'down' Waverley route freight. *W. S. Sellar*

24. *Bottom left:* A striking broadside view of 'A3' No. 60040 *Cameronian* hard at work as it climbs out of Carlisle (near Kingmoor) with the 4.15 pm freight to Edinburgh Millerhill in April 1964. *S. C. Crook*

25. *Above:* Class '5MT' No. 44672 and 'A4' No. 60024 *Kingfisher* provide super power for the heavily loaded 10.15 am Saturdays only Ford train from Ditton junction (Halewood) to Bathgate terminal. The train is seen climbing out of Carlisle past Stainton junction to the bridge over the WCML at Kingmoor. April 1964.

26. *Below:* 'Crab' 2-6-0s were rare visitors to the Waverley route but on a clear November day in 1962 the photographer was lucky enough to catch No. 42836 heading out of Carlisle with a morning freight for Edinburgh. *Both Peter J. Robinson*

27. *Top left:* This broadside view of 'D49' No. 62744 *The Holderness* shows to full advantage the classic proportions of this handsome class of 4-4-0 locomotive designed by Gresley in 1927 for the LNER. The train is the 6.13 pm local service to Hawick and the location near Kingmoor. July 1960. *S. C. Crook*

28. *Bottom left:* Another classic 4-4-0. This time former NBR Class 'D30' No. 62440 *Wandering Willie*. The locomotive is seen in charge of the same train as in the previous picture and in roughly the same location. 1 August 1957. The 'D30', or 'Scott' Class as they were better known, were all named after characters in the novels of Sir Walter Scott, as were the earlier 'D29/2' Class of 4-4-0s. *Robert Leslie*

29. *Above:* The 9.20 am Carlisle—Edinburgh breasting the hump where the Waverley route crossed the LMS main line at Kingmoor. A wisp of steam is visible in the left hand background of the picture. In charge of the train is 'A2' Pacific No. 60512 *Steady Aim*. The date is April 1961. *S. C. Crook*

30. *Left:* Brunthill siding near Kingmoor is the setting for 'A2' Pacific No. 60532 *Blue Peter* as it makes sedate progress with the 5.30 pm goods from Carlisle Canal yard to Aberdeen. 5 August 1961. This famous locomotive has been preserved and is due to make a welcome return to main line running. *Robert Leslie*

31. *Below:* One of Carlisle Canal's famous 'A3' Pacifics No. 60093 *Coronach* is seen on 19 April 1958 in charge of the 1.28 pm Carlisle—Edinburgh train as it moves swiftly through Parkhouse Halt. This station, some three miles from Carlisle, was not open to the general public but served the adjacent RAF maintenance unit. *Robert Leslie*

32. *Top right:* Former NBR 'Glen' Class 4-4-0 No. 62483 *Glen Garry* pulls away from Parkhouse Halt with the 6.30 am Hawick—Carlisle stopper in November 1958. *S. C. Crook*

33. *Bottom right:* 4-4-0 No. 62747 *The Percy* hurries through Harker station at over 50 mph with a return working of a Carlisle—Hawick—Carlisle goods, the date December 1958. This station was closed in 1929 but opened for a brief period during the war. *S. C. Crook*

34. *Top left:* BR standard Class '4MT'
2-6-4T No. 80113, of Hawick shed 64G, pulls out of Longtown
station in August 1965 with the evening Carlisle—Hawick
stopping train. Just south of the station was the junction for the
short NB branch to Gretna which connected with the ex
Caledonian main line at Gretna South junction. *Maurice Burns*

35. *Bottom left:* On 4 April 1959 Class 'V2' 2-6-2 No. 60819
attacks the 1 in 100 gradient near Scotch Dyke with the afternoon
Carlisle—Edinburgh goods. *Robert Leslie*

36. *Above:* At Riddings junction (see next page) is the start of the
branch to Langholm. This branch, which was seven miles in
length, was closed to passenger traffic in 1964 but remained open
for freight workings until September 1967. In this scene we see
Class 'J39' 0-6-0 No. 64964 pulling out of Langholm with the
3.23 pm to Carlisle. 16 April 1960. *Robert Leslie*

37. Three views at Riddings Junction in the middle 1950s:
Top left: The signal box and station seen from the south. *A.J. Robertson*
Bottom left: This photograph emphasises how neat and tidy the station is kept, a tribute to the staff. Class 'J39' 0-6-0 No. 64727 stands in the bay with a Langholm train. Upon arrival from Langholm, No. 64727 would have reversed its train out of the platform in order to run round. It would then have propelled the train back into the bay platform to wait for any passengers from the main line train, due fairly soon.
R. W. Lynn collection

Above: A perfect country railway station scene. In this view looking north Class 'B1' No. 61221 *Sir Alexander Erskine-Hill* has arrived on the 6.35 am Edinburgh Waverley - Carlisle train, while No. 64727 and its train await departure to the busy market town of Langholm. We are indeed fortunate that scenes like this, which have sadly disappeared from our railways, have been preserved in print.   *R. W. Lynn collection*

The next four scenes show the daily Langholm branch goods from Kingmoor.

38. *Top left:* On 21 July 1967 Class '4MT' No. 43106 (now preserved on the Severn Valley Railway) crosses an elegant viaduct as it approaches Langholm with the daily goods from Carlisle Kingmoor.

39. *Bottom left:* Another Class '4MT' No. 43121 departs from Langholm with a very light load and heads for Carlisle. 18 July 1967.

40. *Above:* No. 43121 takes water at Langholm station before returning to Carlisle with the return daily goods working on 17 July 1967. Note the LNER 'Warning to Passengers' signs at the platform end.

41. *Below:* A pleasant reminder of the branch line goods train as 2-6-0 No. 43106 trundles along the Langholm branch near Riddings junction, with the goods from Kingmoor yard.
Four Pictures — Ken Hale

42. *Left:* Back on the main Waverley route as 'A1' Pacific No. 60132 *Marmion* makes a fine sight pulling away from Riddings junction with the 9.20 am Carlisle—Edinburgh train in April 1962 just before the working was dieselised. The viaduct on the right-hand side carries the Langholm branch over Liddel Water. No. 60132 would not have been a regular visitor to the line, being shedded at Heaton (52B).
S. C. Crook

43. *Below:* On a fine August day in 1960 Class 'D34' No. 62488 *Glen Aladale* heads briskly out of Penton with the 12.25 pm (Saturdays only) Hawick—Carlisle local. This fine NB 4-4-0 Class was first introduced in 1913 and as can be seen was still going strong in the 1960s. Penton station building (which can be seen behind the second coach) is happily now privately owned and indeed a section of the 'down' platform still remains intact. *S. C. Crook*

44. Kershopefoot was the boundary station on the Waverley route. On Saturday 25 February 1967 Class '5MT' 4-6-0 No. 44792 enters the station (which was still in England, the border being just north of the station) with an afternoon stopping train from Carlisle to Hawick. This locomotive was obviously deputising for a diesel because by this time all workings on the Waverley had been dieselised. *Gavin Morrison*

45. The same train as in the previous picture (which proves that chasing trains is nothing new!) pulls out of Newcastleton and heads for Hawick. Note the fine repeater signal on the left-hand side of the picture complete with North British post and finial. Newcastleton is the start of the ten mile climb (mainly at 1 in 75) up to Whitrope summit so the fireman of the 'Black Five' is in for some hard work. *Gavin Morrison*

46. *Above:* Class 'B1' 4-6-0
No. 61030 *Nyala* crosses Hermitage
or Sandholm viaduct, just north of
Newcastleton with the 2.12 pm
Carlisle Kingmoor—Edinburgh
Millerhill freight on a very wet
28 July 1965. *C. E. Weston*

47. *Left:* A fine action portrait of
Class 'A1' Pacific No. 60162 *St
Johnstoun* as it leaves Newcastleton
behind and attacks the 1 in 75 up to
Whitrope summit with a Carlisle to
Edinburgh train on 15 April 1961.
These handsome locomotives were
first introduced in 1945 and several
members of the class (including No.
60162) carried the names of the
famous North British Atlantics
designed by W. P. Reid which
worked on the Waverley route from
before the First World War until the
1930s, the Atlantic wheel
arrangement (4-4-2) being especially
suitable for the extreme curvature of
the Waverley route and indeed all the
North British main lines.
Robert Leslie

48. The last northbound train to traverse the whole of the Waverley route was an RCTS railtour from Leeds, hauled by Deltic diesel locomotive No. D9007 *Pinza,* seen climbing away from Newcastleton on Sunday 6 January 1969. *Robert Leslie*

49. Class 'B1' No. 61099 hurries away from Steele Road station with the lightweight 6.13 pm Carlisle—Hawick local train. June 1965. *Peter J. Robinson*

51, 52 and 53. Three scenes, taken on 11 December 1965, of the 2.12 pm Kingmoor—Millerhill goods hauled by Class 'V2' 2-6-2 No. 60976 which are in complete contrast to the previous picture and yet are just as typical of this rugged route. In the top left picture the freight has just left Steele Road and bottom left approaches the photographer about a mile further on. The gully of snow accentuates the rawness of the day. *Two Pictures–Ken Hale*

In the picture above, taken a little further on, a glimmer of light highlights the boiler of the Prairie locomotive. *Dave Lacey*

It should be mentioned here that the above pictures were taken by members of a hardy group of railway photographers known as the Master Neverers Association — MNA for short.

In the final years of BR steam these young men roamed the BR network in search of steam and the master shot or photograph. They were not averse to spending the night hours cleaning locomotives as well as sleeping in PW huts by the lineside in order to obtain this. I think the reader will agree that their considerable efforts were not wasted. They still meet every year on the 11 August, the anniversary of the end of BR steam.

Previous pages

61 *Top left:* A lovely summer day in 1964 as English Electric Type 4 diesel No. D285 drifts down the 1 in 75 grade below Riccarton with an Edinburgh—Carlisle passenger train. Note the sheep pen on the right-hand side of the picture, Cheviot sheep being famous throughout the world. The isolated station at Riccarton Junction can be seen in the right background. This station was for most of its life only accessible by rail. It was only in the last few years of the line that there was road access and this was only by a Forestry Commission track. *Peter J. Robinson*

62. *Bottom left:* Type 2 diesel No. D5383 climbs up to Riccarton Junction with the afternoon Carlisle—Edinburgh passenger train in the late spring of 1965. *Paul Riley*

63. *Right:* The massive Arnton Fell provides a splendid backdrop for Class 'B1' 4-6-0 No. 61349 on 5 June 1965 as it does battle with the 1 in 75 up to Whitrope. The train is the 2.12 pm Kingmoor—Millerhill freight service. *Maurice Burns*

64. *This page:* There have been many fine pictures taken on the Waverley route but this must be amongst the finest. 'V2' No. 60970 is caught by the camera as it approaches Riccarton Junction with the 11.15 am freight from Carlisle to Millerhill. Friday 5 November 1965. *Ken Hale*

RICCARTON JUNCTION — GALASHIELS

Riccarton Junction was a purpose-built railway community of some thirty cottages, entirely cut off from the road until 1963 when the Forestry Commission made available an unmetalled road which joined the B6399 a mile and a half west. It maintained a two-track locomotive shed and depot for the Border Counties line, which came in from the southeast, and for the Whitrope bankers, and provided the junction station amenities. There were boxes at the south and north ends on the 'up' side.

A mile and a tight curve up 1 in 80 brought the line through a loose ashy cutting, over the B6399 from Newcastleton and up to Whitrope summit at 1006 feet. Whitrope Siding box lay on the right at the approach to the tunnel, which was cut through Sandy Edge and needed tiers of brick buttressing to hold back the crumbling rock. The tunnel was 1208 yards long and descended at 1 in 96, steepening to 1 in 72 down the northern approaches; trains could not do much more than 50 mph because of the severe curvatures. The line cut through the ancient dyke called the 'Catrail', fifty miles long and passing through the road just to the east at Robert's Linn Bridge. The moors were dotted with circular stone sheep shelters and new afforestation, and many Iron Age forts. Road, river and rail came together in a slit in the ridge at the foot of Shankend Hill, where a signal box stuck up like a sore thumb on the windswept hillside. Just beyond lay Shankend station, a solid two-storey building on the right, and then the photogenic Shankend viaduct, 597 feet long with fifteen arches of dark grey stone. The farmhouse underneath was painted white and sported a French-style turret.

Road and rail separated, the line following Slitrig Water down 1 in 117-121 to the road at Stobs Castle in a tree-lined valley. Stobs station and box lay in a sheltered sylvan setting; immediately afterwards the line crossed Stobs viaduct, watched on the northern 'up' side by Stobs Camp box. After two miles of twisting along Slitrig Water, it crossed road and river on Lynwood viaduct's six arches of dark grey stone, rounded another spur and ran into Hawick. This important weaving town showed the influence of 'The Auld Alliance' in the many grey French turrets. The main street was built very wide for the markets, but the approaches were narrow, so that they could be barricaded for the Autumn cattle fairs.

The station lay across the River Teviot on the northern edge of town. At the entrance to the cobbled station yard stood a huge timetable board. The station was reached by the six-arched Hawick viaduct, built of brick and edged with stone, and watched over by the very tall brick South box. It was at this signalbox that from NBR days a bell-push on the block shelf rang a bell in the Station Hotel about 150 yards away. This was operated five minutes before every through train was due to arrive. This last mile dropped 1 in 75, giving 'up' trains a formidable start off the platform end. Originally, Hawick was the southern terminus of the Edinburgh & Hawick Railway, which the NB opened on 1 November 1849. (Carlisle was reached twelve years later.) The A7 road bridge close by gave access to the town. There were sidings to serve the woollen mills, and a large shed on the northwest side maintaining some twenty locomotives for the branch lines, bankers for Whitrope, etc. The town's pagan warcry 'Teribus ye Teri Odin' gave the name 'Teribus' to the NB Atlantic No. 906 of 1912.

The line turned northeast up the Teviot valley to Hassendean station which, as 'Hazeldean' in Scott's novel, gave its name to a 1906 Reid Atlantic. The route left the Teviot and passed to the west of the steep Minto hills, through farmlands and sidings at Standhill to the next station and box of Belses (for Ancrum and Lilliesleaf). The building was in the NB's delicate 'pavilion' style reminiscent of the Edinburgh suburbs like Botanical Gardens.

After crossing Ale Water viaduct, the line swung northwest through Greenend sidings and Charlesfield halt (not public). On the eastern skyline rose a column called Baron's Folly and a mausoleum on the battlefield of Ancrum Moor, 1545. These lay on the Roman road Dere Street, which sighted its line on the triple peaks of the Eildon Hills ahead, which gave their name to Trimontium camp at their feet near Melrose. The line entered the Tweed valley and, at Kelso junction and box, the line from Berwick came in from the east. This line, originally double track, opened as far as Kelso (Maxwellheugh) on 1 June 1851 and eventually connected with the NER line from Berwick via Coldstream at Sprouston junction. It lost its passenger service on 15 June 1964 but carried freight until 1968. At Roxburgh, a branch led to Jedburgh, opened as the Jedburgh Railway on 17 July 1856 and taken over by the NB on 3 July 1860.

In a loop in the Tweed near St. Boswells (from St. Boisil, Prior of Melrose) lie the famous ruins of Dryburgh Abbey where Sir Walter Scott was buried. On a hill to the north stand Wallace's statue and the tower of Bemersyde House. At Newtown St. Boswells, the station had a two track shed and a north and south box of jettied construction right beside the 'up' platform. The sidings were a reminder of the enormous sheep fairs. In the boom year of 1920, together with Galashiels, St. Boswells sent over half a million head of sheep and cattle by rail. The station entrance was rebuilt in 1904, commemorated in the stonework.

The line turned west around the red peaks of the Eildons. At Ravenswood junction a single track came in from Berwick on Tweed via Duns and Reston. This got as far as Earlston by 16 November 1863, but the last stretch, the Leaderfoot viaduct of nineteen arches over the Tweed, was finished only on 2 October 1865. The terrible floods of 12 August 1948 destroyed much of the track, and it was closed to passengers, then to freight, from Duns westwards, although the Duns to Reston passenger service survived until 1951 and its goods service until 1966.

The line through the Royal Burgh of Melrose was one of the few straight stretches. The station with its NB lamp standards was beautifully kept and won awards for its flower beds. The ruins of Melrose Abbey, built of rose pink stone, lay right next to the station. Every Christmas week the Freemasons hold a torchlight procession from the Mercat Cross in town to the grave of Robert the Bruce's heart in the nave, which could be seen from passing trains at night.

A couple of miles down 1 in 200 past Darnick sidings took the line to the 278 feet long Redbridge viaduct over the Tweed by the confluence of Gala Water, then to Selkirk junction which was operated by motor points. This branch, some six and a half miles long, began life as the Selkirk & Galashiels Railway on 5 April 1856; it closed to passengers on 10 September 1951. It ran past Abbotsford, Scott's home, after which was named one of Drummond's 4-4-0s of 1876; it wended up the Ettrick Water to Selkirk, where Scott administered justice as Sherrif from 1803 to 1832. Another mile descending 1 in 120-110 brought the Waverley route into the busy industrial weaving town of Galashiels.

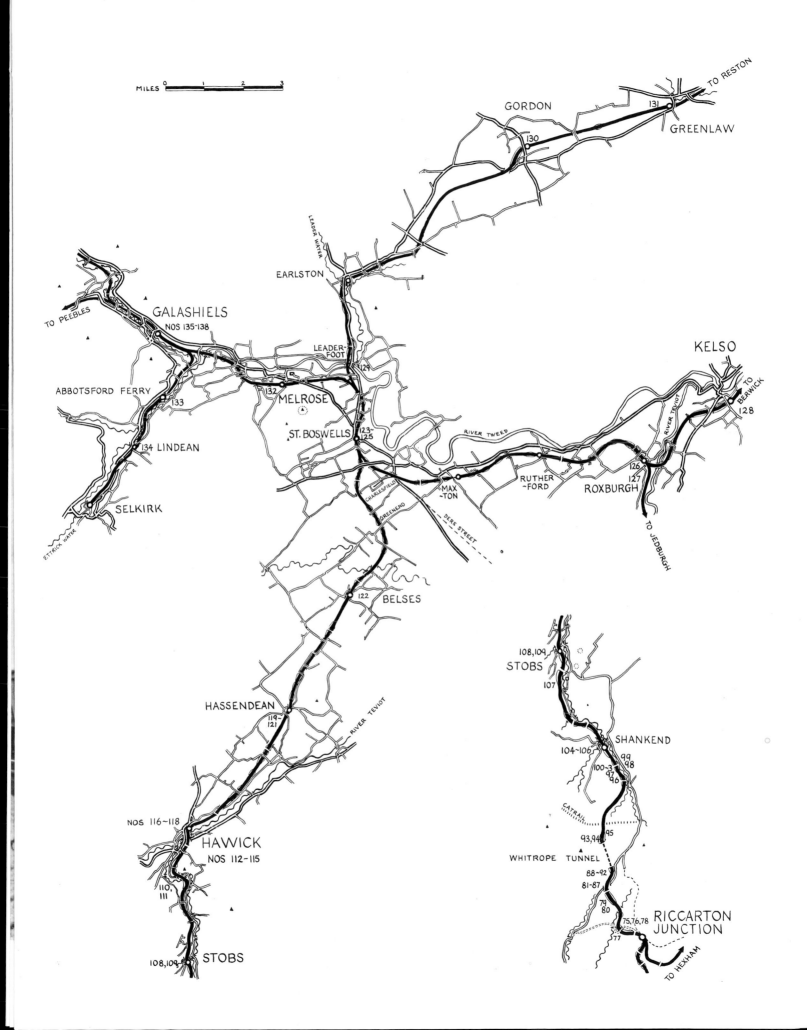

MILES 0 1 2 3

TO RESTON

GORDON
130
131 GREENLAW

LEADER WATER

EARLSTON

KELSO

TO PEEBLES

GALASHIELS
NOS 135-138

LEADER~
FOOT
129

TO BERWICK
128

ABBOTSFORD FERRY
133
132
MELROSE

RIVER TEVIOT

134 LINDEAN

ST. BOSWELLS
123-
125

RIVER TWEED

126
ROXBURGH
127

SELKIRK

ETTRICK WATER

CHARLESFIELD
GREENEND

MAX
~TON

RUTHER
~FORD

DERE STREET

TO JEDBURGH

122 BELSES

STOBS
108,109

107

HASSENDEAN

119~
121

RIVER TEVIOT

SHANKEND
104~106
99
98
100~3
97
96

CATRAIL

NOS 116~118

93,94 95

HAWICK
NOS 112-115

WHITROPE TUNNEL

88~92
81-87

110,
111

79
80

75,76,78

RICCARTON
JUNCTION

77

108,109 STOBS

TO HEXHAM

Previous pages

83. *Top left:* B1 No. 61099 on a northbound pigeon special about half a mile south of Whitrope summit on an August afternoon in 1965. At one time pigeon trains were quite common on BR but like so many other things have disappeared from the scene. *S. C. Crook*

84. *Bottom left:* One of Carlisle Canal's 'A3' 4-6-2s No. 60068 *Sir Visto* makes a splendid sight as it climbs up to Whitrope with the 8.35 am Carlisle—Niddrie goods. 2 December 1961. Niddrie, together with Portobello were Edinburgh's main goods yards until the giant yard at Millerhill was completed in 1962/63. *W. S. Sellar*

85. *Top right:* Class '9F' 2-10-0s were extremely rare visitors to the Waverley route. On 29 December 1965 No. 92114 rounds a tight curve on the approach to Whitrope summit in falling snow with the 11.15 am Carlisle—Millerhill goods. *C. E. Weston*

86. *Bottom right:* 1966 saw the end of steam workings on the Waverley route apart from deputising for diesel failures. One of the last to be run being the B1 special of 3 December 1966. No. 61278 is seen here approaching Whitrope summit in fine style on the northbound journey. *Dave Lacey*

87. *Above:* 'V2' No. 60955 is in charge of the light-weight 6.13 pm Carlisle—Hawick local train in April 1965. The train is about to cross over the B6399 from Newcastleton to Hawick and in a few hundred yards will be over Whitrope summit and can then coast down grade to Hawick, a distance of just over ten miles. *Paul Riley*

88. *Top right:* 'A3' Pacific No. 60057 *Ormonde* passing Whitrope summit on 26 May 1956 with the 2.33 pm Edinburgh—Carlisle train. *Robert Leslie*

89. *Bottom right:* 'J38' 0-6-0 No. 65915, a class rarely seen on the southern end of the Waverley route, passes the lonely Whitrope Siding signal box 1,006 ft above sea level, with a lightweight Hawick—Carlisle goods on 15 April 1961. This sturdy class of 0-6-0 was introduced in 1926 primarily for freight working unlike its contemporary, the Class 'J39' (see picture No. 36), which was designed mainly for local passenger work, the 'J39' having 5'2" driving wheels against the 4'8" wheels of the Class 'J38s'. *Robert Leslie*

90. *Top left:* On 15 June 1965 Class '5MT' No. 45135 approaches Whitrope summit from the north with the 11.40 am Millerhill—Carlisle freight. The southbound climb up to the summit is roughly the same distance as the northbound climb, the first few miles being slightly easier grades but the final half being at 1 in 75, a severe test for any locomotive and its crew. *Paul Riley*

91. *Bottom left:* On the same day as the previous picture Class 'V2' No. 60835 emerges from the 1,208 yard long Whitrope tunnel (the only major one on the route) with a class 1 passenger train. *Paul Riley*

92. *Above:* A most spectacular shot of 'V2' 2-6-2 No. 60970 as it pulls out of Whitrope tunnel on 9 October 1965 with the 8.16 am Millerhill—Carlisle goods. *Ken Hale*

93. *Top left:* A view from the train of the climb to
Whitrope tunnel from the north. The train is the 9.50 am
Edinburgh—Leeds hauled by Class '4MT' 2-6-0 No. 76049
which was put on at Hawick as a replacement for 'V2'
No. 60970 which had faulty injectors. 7 August 1965.
D. C. Williams

94. *Bottom left:* The fireman's view of the climb up to
Whitrope on a very bleak day as 'V2' No. 60976 pounds up
to the summit on 29 December 1965 with the 8.16 am
Millerhill—Kingmoor freight working. *C. E. Weston*

95. *Above:* When the members of the MNA rang up
St. Margaret's depot on 11 December 1965 to find out what
was working the 8.16 am Millerhill—Kingmoor freight that
day they were told No. '4530'. Imagine to their surprise and
delight that instead of 'Black Five' No. 44530 the freight
was worked by the last rebuilt 'Patriot' 4-6-0 No. 45530
seen here hard at work on the 1 in 75 up to Whitrope
summit. *Paul Riley*

96 and 97. *Above and left:* Class 'A2' Pacific No. 60532 *Blue Peter* makes steady progress up to Whitrope summit with a special from Edinburgh—Carlisle on 8 October 1966. This picturesque scene is Shankendshiel some three miles north of the summit.
David E. Gouldthorp

98. *Top right:* A dramatic picture of 'V2' No. 60955 as it climbs away from Shankend with the 5.3 am Millerhill—Carlisle goods on 30 October 1965. *Ken Hale*

99. *Bottom right:* In the summer of 1965 Class 'B1' No. 61076 in charge of a southbound goods makes a very pleasant sight as it climbs the 1 in 75 gradient up to Whitrope summit. The location is near Shankend. Northwards from here to Hawick the line follows closely the course of Slitrig Water. *C. E. Weston*

100. *Right:* The last active 'A3' Pacific (apart from *Flying Scotsman*) was No. 60052 *Prince Palatine*. On what was probably one of its last outings (it was withdrawn a few weeks after this picture was taken) it is seen storming up the 1 in 75 grade at Shankend with the 8.33 am Millerhill—Kingmoor freight on 5 November 1965. I am reliably informed it had a load on of around fifty vans and came by the assembled photographers at an estimated 50 - 55 mph, not bad for an old timer! The cleanliness and white paint on the locomotive was entirely due to the members of the MNA who had spent the night at work on it.
Ken Hale

101, 102 and 103. Three views of track laying near Shankend on the weekend of 17/18 April 1965. In attendance are a pair of Clayton diesels and Class '4MT' 2-6-0 No. 76049. *Paul Riley*

104. *Top left:* Gresley Class 'K3' 2-6-0 No. 61924 and brake van hurry south through Shankend station in the early 1950s. Note the elegant bench complete with the station name, and station lamps mounted on short posts. *Eric Treacy/Millbrook House*

105. *Bottom left:* 'B1' 4-6-0 No. 61244 *Strang Steel* crosses Shankend viaduct on 20 July 1965 with the 12.05 pm Millerhill—Carlisle freight. This dramatic viaduct (which still stands to this day) is 597 feet long and has fifteen arches, and is situated just north of the station. *C. E. Weston*

106. *Above:* Shankend viaduct at its very finest on the afternoon of 31 July 1965. The train is the 1.35 pm Millerhill—Kingmoor goods hauled by 'B1' 4-6-0 No. 61350. *C. E. Weston*

107. *Top left:* 'A3' Pacific *Flying Scotsman* climbs through Stobs cutting, some two miles north of Shankend, with a southbound special. 16 April 1966. *D. C. Williams*

108. *Bottom left:* In the summer of 1962 'B1' 4-6-0 No. 61290 climbs through Stobs station with a southbound freight. Worthy of note are the North British lower quadrant signals.
Eric Treacy/Millbrook House

109. *Above:* Class 'A1' Pacific No. 60160 *Auld Reekie* hurries through Stobs station with an Edinburgh—Carlisle passenger train in the early 1960s. Stobs, as well as being a very picturesque area, (as indeed is nearly all of the Waverley route) also boasts a castle.
Eric Treacy/Millbrook House

110. *Above:* A driver's view of Lynwood viaduct, which crosses the lovely Slitrig Water, a mile south of the famous Scottish border town of Hawick. The train is the 6.50 am Hawick—Carlisle local hauled by 2-6-0 No. 76049 and the date is 5 June 1965. This was the last regular steam hauled passenger working between these famous old towns, the return working being the 6.13 pm off Carlisle. *Maurice Burns*

111. *Top right:* 'A1' Pacific No. 60159 *Bonnie Dundee* crosses the graceful Lynwood viaduct and approaches Hawick with the 3.22 pm Carlisle—Edinburgh train on 2nd September 1960. *W. A. C. Smith*

112. *Bottom right:* 'V2' No. 60824 climbs the 1 in 75 out of Hawick and heads for Carlisle with a heavy freight from Millerhill on a wet summer's day in 1965. *Maurice Burns*

113. *Above:* Type 2 diesel No. 5307 crosses the viaduct over the River Teviot at the southern end of Hawick station with a southbound passenger train in the autumn of 1965. Note the vintage bus. *Paul Riley*

114. *Below:* Another of Carlisle Canal's famous 'A3' Pacifics No. 60079 *Bayardo* restarts the 12.00 pm Edinburgh—Carlisle train up the 1 in 75 out of the sharply curved Hawick station. 1 April 1958. It was not uncommon for southbound trains to be given rear end assistance by the station pilot. *W. S. Sellar*

115 and 116. *Opposite page:* Two views at Hawick of Class 'B1' No. 61349 on the 8.05 am train to Edinburgh in the summer of 1965. In the top view the 4-6-0 is framed by the station footbridge as it waits to depart. In the bottom scene No. 61349 makes a storming start out of the station as it heads north. Although the gradient is not as severe as for southbound trains leaving Hawick nevertheless it is 1 in 150. On the right-hand side is the shed and on the left the viaduct south of the station, (see picture 113) which shows the extreme curvature of the station layout. *Maurice Burns*

117. *Left:* Hawick shed 19 September 1955 with Class 'C16' 4-4-2T No. 67489. These handsome Atlantic tank engines were first introduced in 1915 but were withdrawn by the 1950s. *W. S. Sellar*

118. *Below:* Scott Class 4-4-0 No. 62422 beautifully named *Caleb Balderstone*, and Class 'J36' 0-6-0 No. 65331 in Hawick shed yard on 1 April 1958. These elegant 0-6-0s were introduced by the North British in 1888 and some of them lasted until almost the end of BR steam. *W. S. Sellar*

119. *Top right:* On a wet 23 July 1965 'B1' No. 61191 hurries along between Hawick and Hassendean with the 11.15 am Carlisle–Millerhill class 5 freight. *C. E. Weston*

120. *Bottom right:* 'A2' Pacific No. 60528 *Tudor Minstrel* approaches Hassendean with a special from Manchester–Edinburgh on 23 April 1966. *Maurice Burns*

123. *Above:* Class 'D30' 4-4-0 No. 62432 *Quentin Durward* is on station pilot duties at St. Boswells in April 1958. St. Boswells was the junction for the lines to Kelso (and Berwick) to the north east and Jedburgh to the southeast, the lines parting at Roxburgh junction some eight miles to the east of St. Boswells. Also north of St. Boswells was the junction for the line to Greenlaw which formerly ran to Duns and Reston but was truncated between Greenlaw and Duns by the floods of 12 August 1948. Freight workings carried on to Greenlaw until 1967. *S. C. Crook*

121. *Top left:* A view of Hassendean station, emphasising its rural tranquility. *R. W. Lynn collection*

122. *Bottom left:* Belses station, looking south, in November 1955. Note the 'J36' 0-6-0 and brake van in the sidings opposite the signal box. *C. J. B. Sanderson*

124. *Below:* Class 'D34' 4-4-0 No. 62732 *Dumfries-shire* on shed at St. Boswells. 6 May 1957. *Hugh Ballantyne*

125. *Top left:* 'Glen' Class 4-4-0 No. 62471 is seen at St. Boswells on 4 April 1959 with a Branch Line Society railtour. The end of the shed building is just visible on the right-hand side. The bay platform is for the Kelso service. *W. S. Sellar*

126. *Bottom left:* The same train as in the previous picture only now pausing at Roxburgh junction before heading south down the Jedburgh branch. Note the wonderful array of NB lower quadrant signals. *W. S. Sellar*

127. *Above:* On 14 April 1963 'B1' 4-6-0 No. 61324 crosses Roxburgh viaduct (over the River Teviot) with a SLS/BLS special train from Kelso. *W. S. Sellar*

128. *Below:* Class 'V1' 2-6-2T No. 67630 stands at Kelso station whilst working the 4.05 pm train from St. Boswells to Berwick on Tweed, one of only two trains each way per day on this cross border NBR branch line. 6 May 1957. *Hugh Ballantyne*

129. *Top left:* On 15 May 1958 Class 'J35' 0-6-0 No. 64494 crosses Leaderfoot viaduct with a return daily goods working from Greenlaw to Hawick, the line having originally gone through to Reston.
W. S. Sellar

130 and 131. Two views of the Branch Line Society trip of 4 April 1959, on the branch line to Greenlaw. In the bottom left view *Glen Falloch* pauses at Gordon station and the view top right shows the train at Greenlaw. *W. S. Sellar*

132. *Right:* Shortly after leaving St. Boswells the main line swings due west and arrives at Melrose some three miles further on. Melrose station is shown here on 10 July 1952. While the platforms are quiet, there is a fair amount of traffic visible in the goods yard.

A. G. Ellis

133. *Top left:* Galashiels is four miles to the northwest of Melrose. One mile before reaching that famous old border town was the junction for the branch to Selkirk. No. 62471 with the BLS trip of 4 April 1959 pauses at Abbotsford Ferry, Abbotsford being the birthplace of Sir Walter Scott. A ferry existed to allow people to cross the River Tweed to Sir Walter Scott's house. *W. S. Sellar*

134. *Bottom left:* The same train as in the previous picture only this time at Lindean some two miles from Selkirk. *W. S. Sellar*

135. *Above:* Elegant 'A3' Pacific No. 60043 *Brown Jack* pulls out of Galashiels with an Edinburgh—Carlisle local on 23 April 1960. *W. S. Sellar*

136. *Below:* Galashiels shed on 19 June 1949. Outside the shed is Class 'D34' 4-4-0 No. 62471 *Glen Falloch* and Class 'D30' 4-4-0 No. 62420 *Dominie Sampson. W. A. Camwell*

137. *Left:* 'A4' Pacific No. 60031 *Golden Plover* heads south out of Galashiels on 18 April 1965 with a southbound special. The locomotive shed is clearly seen above the train. *Tim Stephens*

138. *Below:* The 9.50 am Edinburgh to Leeds (via the Settle & Carlisle route) prepares to leave Galashiels on 14 August 1965. This train was a pleasant reminder of pregrouping days when the Midland Railway ran from St. Pancras to Carlisle via the S & C and connected with the NB Waverley route trains to Edinburgh. *D. C. Williams*

GALASHIELS — EDINBURGH

Galashiels station was built in the Scottish manorial style with a huge timetable board outside the booking hall. It was the major coal and water stop and sometimes crews changed here. The extensive sidings for the woollen industry and the sheds lay well to the southeast side of the station, which was squeezed in tiers between the streets on the north bank of Gala Water. The A7 bridge ran diagonally right over the station.

On crossing Gala Water — there were sixteen bridges in fifteen miles — the line came to Kilnknowe junction which was operated by motor points. This was the southern end of the single track Peebles loop opened on 18 June 1866, the northern end being at Hardengreen junction. The loop was closed on 5 February 1962.

At Bowland the station which was closed to passengers in 1953 lay near the junction of the B710 with the A7. At Bowshank, the river made a horseshoe loop round a limb of the hills, and the line cut through a tunnel 249 yards long with a lattice girder bridge at each end. Most of the remaining bridges were of the low humped girder type; the line flipped over the meandering river like a skipping stone and hugged the alluvial terraces each side of the valley floor, rising about 1 in 150 for seven miles to Falahill summit. The deeply eroded Moorfoot hills to the west and the Lammermuirs to the east formed an escarpment known as the Southern Uplands Fault; Gala water followed a snag in the otherwise clean line.

The station at Stow lay on a severe curve. It looked past its box to a roofless ivy-covered church and its Victorian replacement. Just before Fountainhall station was the junction for Lauder, famous for trout fishing in Leader Water. The 'Lauder Light' ran its single track for twelve tortuous miles. It was opened on 2 July 1901 but closed to passengers on 12 September 1932.

The major river Heriot Water came in from the west while the line struggled north following the lesser Gala Water. At Heriot station, the platforms were staggered and linked by the level crossing between them. Another mile took the line to Falahill summit at 880 feet. There were two simple railway cottages, a brick box and a stone water tower on the east side, and sidings for bankers on the west.

Road and rail divided to find their separate ways down the steep escarpment, in many places 1 in 75. The next station of Tynehead was perched on the lip of a deep cutting and the platforms were reached by paths. The line swung sharply west down Borthwick bank, passing a mineral track running north. The pass was guarded by Borthwick Castle and a church with a distinctively angled spire, a fantastic sight in the moonlit winter snows.

After Fushiebridge closed to passengers in 1943, and completely in 1959, Gorebridge station served the area. This station of golden sandstone lay in the fork of the B704 and B6372 and had staggered platforms, with a sun-drenched box on the 'up' side. The gradient eased to 1 in 150, past the Lothian coalmines. Spurs ran right to Arniston colliery and to Lady Victoria pit, well-hidden in the trees.

The line swung west again after the station at Newtongrange, where the booking hall was upstairs, crossing the South Esk on Newbattle viaduct which had twenty-two arches and reached nearly 1,200 feet in length, with the A7 running along in its shadow. It ran past Dalhousie station which closed back in 1908 and came to the re-entry of the Peebles line at Hardengreen junction where there was a signalbox and depot on the left, for the Falahill bankers and the Peebles locomotives. This northern leg was opened on 4 July 1855. In the final years the Penicuik branch survived which kept the Hardengreen to Hawthornden section open. The next junction, Glenesk, at Eskbank was for a spur to Dalkeith station, closed long ago, and the extension to the Duke of Buccleuch's collieries at Smeaton, etc. After Esbkank & Dalkeith station, the Waverley joined the original Edinburgh & Dalkeith Railway, which ran from St. Leonards on the Scottish gauge of 4'6". First opened as a horse-drawn mineral line to carry coal to 'Auld Reekie' in the difficult winter months, it also took passengers from 2 June 1832, earning the nickname, 'The Innocent Railway' on its reputation for safety. It was bought by the NB in October 1845, re-gauged and linked to the new Berwick line into Edinburgh North Bridge (later General, then Waverley), reopening on 14 July 1847 for passengers.

The next junction, coming from Bilston Glen colliery to the west, sent coal to the recently extended yards at Millerhill and thence to Cockenzie power station on the coast. At Niddrie South junction, a spur onto the Edinburgh Circle followed the Innocent Railway, while the Waverley rose over one spur from the East Coast main line, joined the Circle northward at Niddrie North junction, and passed under a second spur, then turned west dropping 1 in 80 through an inconspicuous cutting.

At Portobello East junction there was a complex of marshalling yards on the north side as far as West junction. Skirting the northern flank of the mountain Arthur's Seat, it passed the junction of the NB spur to Leith and Granton Docks; once there had been plans to build an 'Atmospheric' railway there. The docks' loop rejoined opposite Holyrood Palace, enclosing St. Margarets shed in its triangle. The line rose through St. Margarets (or Calton) twin tunnels under Calton Hill on which stands the Scottish Office, built onto Calton Gaol, and 'Scotland's Shame', a half-finished monument to the fallen in the Peninsular Wars.

Rising 1 in 78, it reached the many tracks running into Waverley station. The railway and Prince's Street Gardens beyond, where rises the monument to Sir Walter Scott, were laid on the site of Nor'Loch at the foot of Edinburgh Castle Rock, which was drained in the 19th century. The station was rebuilt, no higher than thirty feet above track level to comply with the law of 'Ancient Lights', and extended over the site of Waverley Market in the period 1892 — 1900. The North Bridge which was formerly stone and round-arched, was also rebuilt in wide graceful metal arches, and the North British Hotel with its conspicuous clocktower was erected in 1902.

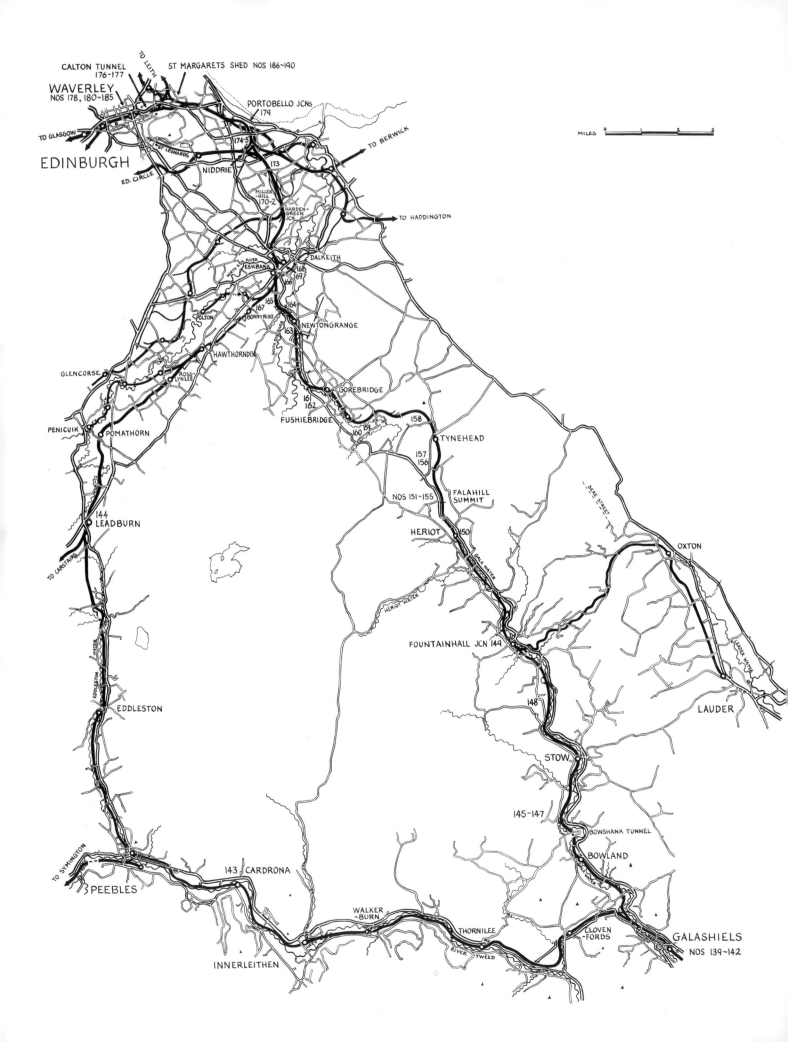

139. *Above:* Class 'B1' 4-6-0 No. 61191 eases through Galashiels with an 'up' parcels train on a wet and windy day in the mid 1950s. Today nothing remains of the station but the distinctive road bridge which carries the link road between the A72 and A6091 is still to be seen. Note the fine old carriage in the siding on the right. *Eric Treacy/Millbrook House*

140. *Right:* A delightful winter scene at Galashiels as Class 'J36' 0-6-0 No. 65327 pauses during snow clearing activities on 8 February 1958. *W. S. Sellar*

Previous pages

141 and 142. *Left:* Two scenes taken on the same day in the mid 1950s which show that the Waverley route, even prior to the completion of Millerhill yard in the early 1960s, always had a fair amount of freight traffic. In the top view Class 'K3' 2-6-0 No. 61900 has just arrived at the northern end of Galashiels station with a haul of coal empties for return to the Lothian pits and is held by the signals to allow through (bottom picture) sister engine No. 61876 in charge of a northbound van train.
Two Pictures Eric Treacy/Millbrook House

Just north of Galashiels was the junction for the line to Peebles which formed a loop line by rejoining the Waverley route at Hardengreen junction some seven miles from Edinburgh.

143. *Top right:* NBR Reid designed 'J37' 0-6-0 No. 64577 runs tender first across the River Tweed at Cardrona with the daily pick-up goods from Peebles to Galashiels. 25 August 1960. *Hugh Ballantyne*

144. *Bottom right:* Conversation piece at Leadburn as the driver of the Edinburgh to Galashiels via Peebles train enjoys a wintry chat with a member of the station staff before heading south. The train is hauled by St. Margarets 'B1' No. 61332 and the date is 8 February 1958. *W. S. Sellar*

145. *Above:* After leaving Galashiels the Waverley line ran for some fifteen miles through the scenic valley of the Gala Water which it crossed many times. On 3 September 1966 a pair of Clayton Class 17 diesels Nos. D8565 and D8566 plus a Type 4 English Electric diesel No. D398 triple head a northbound freight between Bowland and Stow. *Les Nixon*

146 and 147. *Right:* On the same day as the previous picture 'V2' 2-6-2 No. 60836 is seen (above) heading out of Bowshank tunnel and (below) skirting the Gala Water near Stow with the northbound *Granite City* from Euston to Aberdeen.
Two Pictures Les Nixon

179. This next picture has been taken slightly out of journey order for obvious technical reasons. 'Scott' Class 4-4-0 No. 62437 *Adam Woodcock* having gained the Waverley route just south of Portobello East junction, makes a beautiful sight as it climbs up to Niddrie North junction with a very unusual rake of wagons and heads south on 29 August 1956. The Waverley route leaves the East Coast main line at Portobello East junction which can be seen at the back of the train. There is much to enjoy in this splendid railway portrait.
Gavin Morrison

184. *Left:* 'A1' No. 60152 *Holyrood* makes a beautiful sight as it pulls out of Waverley in 1960 with the mid-day train to Carlisle. The name *Holyrood* was previously borne by NB 4-4-2 No. 904.
Eric Treacy/Millbrook House

185. *Above:* A classic picture taken in the 1950s. 'A3' Pacific No. 60068 *Sir Visto* makes a spirited start out of Waverley station with the mid-day express for Carlisle.
Eric Treacy/Millbrook House

188 and 189. *Right:* A row of tank engines and a 'V2' No. 60919 are seen inside the main shed building. The tank locomotives are BR Class '4MT' 2-6-4T Nos. 80055, 80113, 80006 and 80114, together with Fairbairn 2-6-4Ts Nos. 42273 and 42128. In the 1950s although there were no Pacifics at St. Margarets (the A3s were shedded at Carlisle Canal) there were many other types of LNER locomotives shedded there as well as some former NB classes. It should be added that Edinburgh Haymarket Pacifics were regular visitors to the Waverley route. *Roger Siviter*

186. *Top left:* St. Margarets shed (64A) was the principal supplier of motive power on the northern end of the Waverley route. Indeed it remained so until the end of steam working on the route. In its heyday it had allocation of around 200 engines but by the end in the autumn of 1966 this had dwindled to less than a dozen. On 17 July 1965 celebrated 'A4' Pacific No. 60007 *Sir Nigel Gresley* is seen alongside 'B1' 4-6-0 No. 61344. Behind *Sir Nigel* is an unidentified A4. *Ken Hale*

187. *Bottom left:* Class '5MTs' Nos. 45477, 44791 and an English Electric type 4 diesel bask in the summer sunshine of June 1966. *Roger Siviter*

190. Class 'V2' 2-6-2 No. 60955, complete with shed code poses at St. Margarets on 19 June 1966. Apart from the main shed building there was an open round-house where the smaller tank engines were stabled. *Roger Siviter*

SCOTTISH
BORDERS
LIBRARY
SERVICE